THE C

Kingsway Pocketbooks

The Compassionate Father

Floyd McClung Jr

KINGSWAY PUBLICATIONS
EASTBOURNE

Copyright © Floyd McClung 1985

This edition first published 1991

All rights reserved.
No part of this publication may be reproduced or
transmitted in any form or by any means, electronic
or mechanical, including photocopy, recording, or any
information storage and retrieval system, without
permission in writing from the publisher.

Taken from *The Father Heart of God*

Unless otherwise indicated, biblical quotations are from the
Revised Standard Version copyrighted 1946, 1952, ©
1971, 1973 by the Division of Education and Ministry
of the National Council of the Churches of Christ in the USA.

Cover design by Ron Bryant-Funnell

British Library Cataloguing in Publication Data
McClung, Floyd
 The Compassionate Father
 1. Christian doctrine. God. Love
 I. Title
 231.6

ISBN 0-86065-892-9

Printed in Great Britain for
KINGSWAY PUBLICATIONS LTD
1 St Anne's Road, Eastbourne, E. Sussex BN21 3UN by
Richard Clay Ltd, Bungay, Suffolk.

Contents

1. The Broken Heart of God — 7
2. The Waiting Father — 20
3. Why God Heals Wounded Hearts — 33
4. How God Heals Wounded Hearts — 43

I

The Broken Heart of God

I had spent a long week lecturing and counselling in Norway and I was exhausted. I love being with people, but by the end of a week consisting of eighteen-hour days, I just wanted to be alone. I was 'people tired'.

As I climbed out of the taxi in front of Oslo's International Airport, I sent a silent prayer heavenward. My request was simple enough: all I wanted was a seat to myself on the aeroplane, with a little extra legroom (for my two metre frame) to spread out and rest on the three-hour flight back to Amsterdam.

Walking down the centre aisle of the plane, slightly stooped over to avoid hitting my head on the ceiling, I found an empty row of seats, by a bulkhead no less, so that meant extra legroom and a quiet flight back to Schiphol Airport. I smiled to myself smugly as I turned to sit down in the aisle seat, thinking how good God was to answer my prayer for a little rest and peace. 'God understands how tired I am,' I thought.

As I turned to take my seat, a smiling, rather

dishevelled man came up the aisle and greeted me boisterously. 'Hi! You an American?'

'Yes . . . yes I am,' I said with some lack of enthusiasm, as I continued to sit down. I chose the aisle seat thinking it would be harder for anyone to sit by me since they would have to step over my long legs! I heard the man who greeted me sit down in the seat behind me, but I paid him no attention as I settled down to do a little reading.

After a few minutes his head came around the corner. 'Whatcha reading?' he asked as he peered over my shoulder. 'My Bible,' I replied a bit impatiently. Couldn't he see I wanted to be alone? I settled back in my seat, but a few minutes later the same pair of eyes were again looking over the top of my seat. 'What kind of work do you do?' he asked.

Not wanting to get involved in a long conversation, I decided to make my answer brief. 'A kind of social work,' I said, hoping he wouldn't be interested. It bothered me a little that I was verging on not telling the truth, but I dared not tell him I was involved in helping needy people in the inner city of Amsterdam. That would be sure to provoke more questions.

'Mind if I sit by you?' he asked as he stepped over my crossed legs. He seemed to be oblivious to my efforts to avoid talking to him. He turned to face me and he reeked of alcohol. He spat as he spoke, sending a fine spray all over my face.

I was deeply irritated by this man's obnoxiousness. Couldn't he see I wanted to be alone? All my plans for a quiet morning were destroyed by his insensitivity. 'Oh God,' I groaned inwardly, 'please help me.' The conversation moved slowly at first. I answered a few questions about our work in Amsterdam, and began to wonder why this man wanted so desperately to talk to someone. As the conversation unfolded it dawned on me that perhaps I was the one who was being insensitive.

'My wife was like you,' he said after a while. 'She prayed with our children, sang to them and took them to church. In fact,' he said slowly, his eyes misting over, 'she was the only real friend I ever had.'

'Had?' I asked. 'Why are you referring to her in that way?'

'She's gone.' By this time the tears were beginning to trickle down his cheeks. 'She died three months ago giving birth to our fifth child. Why?' he gasped, 'Why did your caring God take my wife away? She was so good. Why not me? Why her? And now the government says I'm not fit to care for my own children, and they're gone too!'

I reached out and took his hand and we wept together. How selfish, how insensitive I had been. I had only been thinking of my need for a little rest when someone like this man desperately needed a friend. He filled in the rest of the story for me. After his wife died, a government appointed social worker recommended that the children be cared for by the state. He was so overwhelmed by grief that he couldn't work, so he also lost his job. In just a few weeks he had lost everything, his wife, his children and his work. It was December so he had decided to leave; he couldn't bear the thought of being at home alone for Christmas without his wife or children, and he was literally trying to drown his sorrows in alcohol.

He was almost too bitter to be comforted. He had grown up with four different step-fathers and he never knew his real dad. All of them were hard men. When I mentioned God he reacted bitterly. 'God?' he said. 'I think if there is a God he must be a cruel monster! Why did your loving God do this to me?'

As I flew on the aeroplane with that wounded, hurt man, I was reminded again that many people in our world have no understanding of a loving God – a God who is a loving Father. To speak of a loving God, a God who is a Father, only evokes pain for them. And anger. To speak of the father heart of God to these people, without empathizing with their pain, verges on cruelty. The only way I could be a friend to that man, on the trip from Oslo to Amsterdam, was to *be* God's love to him. I didn't try to give pat answers. There were none. I just let him be angry and then poured some oil on his wounds. He wanted to believe in God, but deep inside his sense of justice had been violated. He needed someone to say that it was okay for him to be angry, and to tell him that God was angry too. By the time I had listened and cared and wept with him, he was ready to hear me say that God was more hurt than he was by what had happened to his wife and family.

No one had ever told him that God has a broken heart.

He listened in silence as I explained that God's creation was so marred by sin and selfishness, that it is completely different now from how he created it. It is fallen. It is not normal. The question that he asked, of course, and that all of us ask at one time or another is, why? Why does God allow it to happen? Why doesn't he intervene? Why did he create something that could become fallen and marred? If he is a loving Father, why does he allow all the suffering and injustice that goes on in our world?

I tried to help him with the answers to these questions that had helped me, but I would greatly stress that before we ever try to answer these questions with our 'head' we must feel them with our heart. It is profoundly insensitive to treat those kinds of questions merely as some kind of intellectual exercise. If we do feel deeply about suffering and are sensitive to the suffering of others, then I believe we can point in the right direction to show the answers. We must remember it is out of hurt, not just rebellion, that some people deny God's existence. When they experience suffering they lash out at God. It is incomprehensible to them that he could be good yet tolerate evil in his universe. So they deny his existence.

But lashing out at God obviously does not solve the problem. If there is no personal infinite God, *suffering loses all meaning*. If there is no God, man is just a complex product of chance, and 'suffering' is just the result of an evolutionary process, a physical-chemical problem of development. It is perhaps a case of the survival of the fittest, but if there is no God, there are no moral absolutes, and therefore no basis to say that any form of suffering is morally wrong. By denying his existence we are denying any meaning to life itself, and therefore we are saying that it really makes no difference whether people suffer or not. We could not even ask the question, 'Why do the innocent suffer?' because there is no such thing as innocence. Innocence implies guilt, and guilt implies that some things are absolutely, morally wrong.

I believe suffering is wrong, and the very fact that God does exist allows us to say that so emphatically. But that brings us to another important consideration.

How does God feel about suffering and evil in his creation? The Bible answers that question very directly. It says that it brings great sorrow to his heart.

'The Lord saw that the wickedness of man was great in the earth, and that every imagination of the thoughts of his heart was only evil continually. And the Lord was sorry that he had made man on the earth, and it grieved him to his heart' (Gen 6:5,6).

We have asked questions up to this point that deal with the justice of God. Now let's turn it around and ask questions about *our* response to evil and suffering. Do we react just as deeply as God does to evil in the world? More importantly, how do we react to evil in our own lives? Have we shared the sorrow of God's heart over sin, and what it does to bring destruction to all that it touches? It is hypocritical to say we care about suffering in the world, if we have not grieved deeply over the suffering our own selfishness has brought to God and to others.

Sin grieves God's heart. My sin and your sin has brought great sorrow to his heart. Because this is not just an intellectual exercise, and I assume you would not be reading a book like this, unless you were committed to the pursuit of truth with real integrity, may I suggest that you stop now and think about this very important question? If you have never experienced God's sorrow over sin, why don't you ask him to bring true sorrow to your heart over sin and its results?

We can never experience complete healing for our emotional wounds, or fully receive the Father's love unless we share God's sorrow over sin and selfishness. The Bible teaches that there is a difference between godly sorrow and worldly sorrow over sin. Paul wrote to the Corinthian Christians and said, 'I rejoice, not because you were grieved, but because you were grieved into repenting, for you felt a godly grief, so that you suffered no loss through us. For godly grief produces a repentance that leads to salvation and brings no regret, but worldly grief produces death (2 Corinthians 7:9–10).

Repentance is not just being sorry, it is being sorry

enough to stop doing wrong. Godly sorrow is not just confessing our sins. If we confess our sins, but keep on committing them, we have not really experienced godly grief. Nor is repentance just feeling bad about what we have done. Sometimes we feel bad simply because we have been caught, or we feel bad if we have to stop sinning, but godly sorrow is not based on feelings or selfish motives. Godly sorrow is based on how sin hurts God and others. Godly sorrow produces a change in our attitude to sin itself. We begin to hate sin and love goodness.

Godly sorrow also results in a new respect for God and his laws. His laws are very reasonable when you think about them: do not kill, do not steal, do not lie, do not take other people's husbands or wives, and so on. To obey these laws is not living by an outside, imposed morality, but it is living the way we were created to live. Cars are 'created' to drive on roads – not through canals, over fields or off the sides of mountains; they were made to be powered by petrol, not water or coca-cola. Some people might say that it's no fun unless you can drive cars in lakes and off the sides of mountains, but nevertheless they were not created to be driven that way! Unless you use a car for its intended purpose you will destroy it.

So it is with us. God created us to love one another, to be kind, unselfish, forgiving, honest, loyal to our husbands and wives, and to recognize him and live in fellowship with him. Actually, the very heart and meaning of our existence is found in loving God. If we do love God, obeying his laws will come very naturally. We should not attempt to obey God's laws in order to go to heaven, or escape going to hell, or to be well respected, or get something from God. We should obey God's laws because he loves us and we want to respond to his love by pleasing him with our words and actions. Obedience is a *love response* to God!

In Amsterdam there are laws against a man beating his wife. Now, I do not beat my wife, nor do I have to have a policeman follow me around with a gun at my back, saying: 'I'm right behind you so you had better not beat your wife!' Why don't I beat my wife? Is it fear of the law that motivates me? No! It is *love*.

Sharing God's broken heart also frees us to hate what he hates, without feeling that we have lost our integrity. Many people hate God because of religion. They have associated him with all the junk and hypocrisy they have seen in Christianity, and they have rejected him as well as the junk.

Most agnostics have given up on God because of the false image of God or Christ given by the church. I think the Australians are a classic example of this. Some people, even some Australians themselves, will tell you that most Australians couldn't care less about God. But I don't believe that. They have not simply rejected God, they have rejected false images of God. The god they reject, I reject also.

When Bob Hawke became Prime Minister of Australia he gave an interview, during which he said he had learned to care about the working man from his father's deep care for the working class, which was derived from his belief in the fatherhood of God. But Bob Hawke threw out his faith in God because of a disillusioning experience with the church while attending a conference in India.

John Smith, an Australian friend, said in a University mission lecture, that there are three false images of God that Australians have rejected, thinking they have rejected the God of the Bible:

1. The God of indifference

2. The God of privilege and prosperity
3. The God of arbitrary judgement.

Early Americans went to America because of their convictions, but Australians were sent to Australia *for* their convictions. One writer suggested that sending unwanted criminals from England to Australia was like sending your sewage as far away as possible from your house! Some men were sent for as little as stealing a loaf of bread. Australia was seen as a giant penal colony. Many of the prison wardens were priests and ministers. Can you imagine how most men felt about God if they were sent unjustly to an Australian prison and their sentence was enforced by a priest or minister? As John Smith says, 'Australia has a history that causes many not to believe in God, when really they should not believe in man!'

If you have been offended by hypocrisy in the church, or if you have rejected an arbitrary God that gives men laws they cannot keep and then sends them to hell for not keeping them, or if you are angry about injustice and poverty and have been presented with a God who does not care, then you can start again without losing your integrity. You have not been rejecting the God of the Bible. You have not rejected Jesus Christ!

The God of the Bible, the God who has revealed himself in Jesus Christ, hates hypocrisy. He is angry at injustice. The difference between God and us is not anger over injustice, but the fact that he is absolutely just and we are not.

People, like the man I met on the aeroplane, get angry at God because they are hurt – either through personal disappointment or through reaction to injustice in the world around them. But a humble, honest man cannot take out his anger permanently on

God because he must eventually acknowledge that he is guilty of the very things he accuses God of doing! We have all committed the same sins as the greatest criminals in history. We don't want to see ourselves that way, and of course we have not necessarily done it to the same degree, nor have we necessarily let our selfishness dominate us to the same extent, but in word or thought, and sometimes in deed, we express the same sins that we condemn in others. We condemn Hitler ruthlessly, but are we just as ruthless in dealing with hatred in our own hearts? 'I don't hate the Jews,' you may say. But is there someone you hate? One of your neighbours perhaps? Or a fellow student? Someone you work with? If we have *hated* someone, anyone, it is the very same attitude that motivated Hitler.

A proud man keeps on accusing God, because he refuses to admit his own guilt. To deal with evil in the world we must begin with ourselves. If we don't accept our own responsibility for evil we will eventually reject God's explanation for good and evil, and come up with a reason or philosophy that excuses us personally from bowing before him and acknowledging his right to rule over our lives.

If we believe in God, but still accuse him of being unjust, we have never humbled ourselves to the extent that we have been able to see how our selfishness has brought grief to his heart.

The heart of God is broken. Sin has broken his heart. My sin and your sin, and the sin of the whole world. But God didn't only grieve over sin. He did something about it. Sin is the most expensive thing in the universe and God paid the price. He gave his own Son as a sacrifice to atone for the sins of the whole world. Man deserves to be punished for breaking God's laws, but

God sent his Son to take the punishment we deserve.

If you are a person who suffers from a low self image, or if you are wounded emotionally, you face a great temptation to become self-centred. It is very easy to spend a lot of time feeling sorry for yourself, or thinking about your needs. Because of this, it is very important that you face the dangers of self-centredness honestly, and choose to put God at the centre of your life. You must aim to be more concerned about the pain God feels in his heart over man's selfishness, than the hurts you feel. By choosing to put God first in your life, you can break out of the patterns of manipulation, or self-pity, or fear that plague you. God longs for you to be healed of these hurts and the patterns they bring, but that cannot happen unless you replace yourself, as the centre of your life, with him as your Creator and heavenly Father.

God did not create us to live a selfish life, but to serve him and others. When we surrender to God we are set free to love others and ourselves, not in a selfish way, but with the same love that God has for us. He created us and cares for us – we are precious to him. As we know this kind of love, it frees us from being controlled by our own needs. Loving others, from a heart that is secure, keeps our love pure and untainted from manipulation and selfishness.

God's heart is broken by pride, hatred, bitterness, dishonesty, greed, and all other forms of selfishness. But in the same way *our* honesty, forgiveness, love, unselfishness and a desire to please him bring great joy to his heart – even more so because of all the selfishness in the world.

Have you ever experienced godly sorrow over sin? Let your anger turn to sorrow. Anger won't change you, but experiencing godly sorrow will. If you have never allowed your heart to be broken, then ask God to reveal to you your heart as he sees it. I am not talking about introspection, that is, looking into your past in a morbid way that produces condemnation, or a sense of failure. I am talking about hating sin the way God hates it, because you can see how destructive it is.

God's heart is broken over sin, and if you want to receive the Father's love, you must not presume on his kindness or breezily take him for granted. If my children want to experience my love when they have done something wrong, they don't do it by ignoring their wrong actions or taking my forgiveness for granted. Because I love them I want to make sure they are not being indifferent about what they have done. I long to put my arms around them and love them, but I love them enough to lead them to true repentance of things they do wrong. When they have been disobedient, or selfish, I take time to make sure they understand what they have done and why it is wrong, and then help them respond appropriately. When they acknowledge they are wrong and express genuine sorrow, then my love can be *received*. I give it regardless, but I have learned that when they are guilty for doing something they know is wrong, they are not really free to receive or enjoy my love and acceptance. I keep on giving it even though they are guilty, but because I love them I am not satisfied until they have received my love.

Many times we do things that are wrong because we are hurt, but that does not excuse us. Even if others have wronged us, we must deal with our attitudes and actions. Do we want to receive the Father's love? It will flood our minds and souls if we simply accept responsibility for what we have done or said or thought, and ask God for forgiveness. When we know we are wrong, we should take time to allow God to work in our hearts. We must not gloss over sin, no matter how small it seems. When we have done this *then* we can go on to receive his love.

Doing our part in this way makes it possible for us to receive the Father's love in full measure. I cannot heal myself, only God can do that. But I can acknowledge when I am wrong in a situation so that my focus is shifted away from blaming others, or justifying and pitying myself. When I do that, my focus naturally shifts to God. Then everything else can be right.

There was once a little boy who tore out a picture of the world from a Christian magazine, cut it into pieces and then tried to put it back together again. He eventually went in tears to his father because he couldn't put the world together! The father had watched his son and knew that on the other side of the picture of the world was a picture of Jesus. Then he helped his son turn over each piece of paper, keeping it in the same position, explaining to him that when Jesus is in the right place, then we can put the world together.

The Father's heart is broken over sin. If we allow our hearts to be broken with the things that break his heart, then he will be right at the centre of our lives. Then and only then can the world be put back together again.

2

The Waiting Father

They say that the first time Sawat went to the top floor of the hotel, he was shocked. He had never dreamed it would be like this. Every room had a window facing into the hallway and in every room sat a girl. Some looked older and they were smiling and laughing, but many of them were just twelve or thirteen years old – some even younger. They looked nervous, even frightened.

It was Sawat's first venture into Bangkok's world of prostitution. It all began innocently enough, but soon he was caught up in it like a small piece of wood in a raging river. It was too powerful for him, too swift, and the current too strong.

Soon he was selling opium to customers and propositioning tourists in the hotels. He even went so low as to actually help buy and sell young girls, some of them only nine and ten years old. It was a nasty business, and he was one of the most important of the young 'business men'.

Sawat became a central figure in one of the world's largest and most loathsome trades: Thailand's sex

THE WAITING FATHER

industry. It is estimated that over 10% of all girls in Thailand end up in prostitution. The top floors of most hotels are used by them, as are the back rooms of many bars. Though the practice is discouraged by the Royal Family, many poorer rural families sell their young daughters to pay off family debts. Who knows what happens to many of these frightened ten-year-olds when they have outlived their usefulness?

Sawat disgraced his family and dishonoured his father's name. He had come to Bangkok to escape the dullness of village life. He found excitement, and while he prospered in this sordid life, he was popular. But then the bottom dropped out of his world. He hit a string of bad luck: he was robbed and while trying to climb back to the top, he was arrested. Everything went wrong. The word spread in the underworld that he was a police spy. He finally ended up living in a shanty by the city rubbish dump.

Sitting in his little shack, he thought about his family, especially his father. He remembered the parting words of his father, a simple Christian man from a small village in the south, near the Malaysian border: 'I am waiting for you.' Would his father *still* be waiting for him after all he had done to dishonour the family name? Would he receive him home after disregarding all he had been taught about God's love? Word had long ago filtered back to his village about his life of crime and sin.

Finally, he devised a plan.

'Dear Father,' he wrote, 'I want to come home, but I don't know if you will receive me after all that I have done. I have sinned greatly, Father. Please forgive me. On Saturday night I will be on the train which goes through our village. If you are still waiting for me will you tie a piece of cloth on the po tree in front of our house?'

During the train ride he thought over his life of evil. He knew his father had every right to refuse to see him. As the train finally neared the village he was filled with anxiety. What would he do if there was no white piece of cloth on the po tree?

Sitting opposite Sawat was a kind stranger who noticed how nervous his fellow-passenger had become. Finally, Sawat could stand the pressure no longer. The story burst out in a torrent of words. He told the man everything. As they entered the village, Sawat said, 'Oh, sir, I cannot bear to look. Can you watch for me? What if my father will not receive me back home?'

Sawat buried his face between his knees. 'Do you see it sir? It's the only house with a po tree.'

'Young man, your father did not hang *one* piece of cloth . . . look! He has covered the whole tree with pieces of white cloth!' He could hardly believe his eyes. There was the tree, covered, and in the front yard his old father was dancing up and down, joyously waving a piece of white cloth! His father ran beside the train, and when it stopped at the little station he threw his arms around his son, embracing him with tears of joy. 'I've been waiting for you,' he exclaimed!

★ ★ ★

A man had two sons. When the younger told his father, 'I want my share of your estate now, instead of waiting until you die,' his father agreed to divide his wealth between his sons.

A few days later this younger son packed all his belongings and took a trip to a distant land, and there wasted all his money on parties and prostitutes. About the time his money was gone a great famine swept over the land, and he began to starve.

He persuaded a local farmer to hire him to feed his pigs. The boy became so hungry that even the pods he was feeding the swine looked good to him. And no one gave him anything.

When he finally came to his senses, he said to himself, 'At home even the hired men have enough and to spare, and here I am, dying of hunger! I will go home to my father and say, "Father, I have sinned against both heaven and you, and am no longer worthy of being called your son. Please take me on as a hired man".'

So he returned home to his father. And while he was still a long distance away, his father saw him coming, and was filled with loving pity and ran and embraced him and kissed him.

His son said to him, 'Father, I have sinned against heaven and you, and am not worthy of being called your son'.

But his father said to the slaves, 'Quick! Bring the finest robe in the house and put it on him. And a jewelled ring for his finger, and shoes. And kill the calf we have in the fattening pen. We must celebrate with a feast. For this son of mine was dead and has returned to life. He was lost and is found'. So the party began. (Lk 15:11–24 TLB)

What a beautiful picture of God these two stories paint for us. The biblical story is often called 'The Prodigal Son', but I think it would be better titled 'The Waiting Father'. There are three aspects of the character of the father in both stories, particularly the biblical parable, that help us understand the father heart of God.

He loved his son enough to let him leave home. He had spent so long preparing his son for adulthood. In the Jewish tradition this meant many hours of teaching him the laws of God. Though he knew what kind of misfortune could befall his younger son, and though he tried to prepare him to be a righteous and responsible member of the Jewish congregation and community, he wisely allowed his son to go, without protest or pressure.

This father understood the purpose of discipline and training. More than outward obedience, he wanted to win the heart of his young son. Now that his son had reached the age where he could ask for his part of the family wealth, as Jewish tradition allowed, the father did not dissent even though it seemed callous and presumptuous of his headstrong son to demand his share of the family wealth at such a young age.

The father was creating the possibility for true relationship through his willingness to allow his son this freedom. Though inwardly he grieved over his son, he did not try to force a relationship with him. He simply made himself available to serve his son as he had always done. He did not give his son this amount of freedom because he agreed with him, but because he loved him and because he was wise enough to wait for his son to want that relationship. He had spent years instructing him in the way he should go. He had spent hundreds of hours teaching him the wisdom found in God's laws. He had been cultivating a friendship with his young son since he was born.

Now the son must choose.

And the father let him go. He knew that to force him to stay against his will was to demand outward conformity without heart relationship. He understood God enough to know that you could live by the law of Moses, and at the same time your heart could be worshipping and longing for other gods. No, he wanted a relationship with his son more than forced obedience, but he must wait until he was ready for that. He would pray and he would wait. His heart would follow his son, but he must wait for him to come back home.

For a father to respond in this way to his rebellious son shows how much this father understood the heart of God. God sovereignly chose to give man free will, and when he did that he took the risk of being rejected. God did not want 'religion' – that is, an impersonal and involuntary obedience to a set of rules. He wanted heart relationship with those whom he created. There is always a risk in giving people freedom of choice, but without that risk there is no true heart relationship. It is not that he wants people to choose against him, but any other solution than our personal freedom would be a violation of true relationship.

This kind of freedom can be violated if we do not give other people the same freedom God gives us. For us to try to force conformity, belief, or obedience, by pressure, threats, rules, withdrawing friendship, making demands or anything else, is to destroy the very heart of Christianity. It is to destroy the grace of God and enter into a religious legalism.

All too often those who are insecure tend to find their security in outward conformity to religious rules, or in the approval of people, rather than putting their security in their personal relationship with Jesus Christ because of his death on the cross.

He loved his son so deeply that he watched every day for him to return home. There is a story told about a man who came every night to a large auditorium to hear a famous evangelist preach the gospel. Night after night he came, yet he was unmoved in his firm conviction that there was no reason to go forward in response to the appeals to make a public commitment to Jesus Christ. 'I can pray right here where I'm sitting,' thought the man. And each night he returned to hear more, always sitting in the same place. Night after night a polite young usher approached the well-to-do visitor and asked him if he would like to go forward to make a public commitment to follow Jesus Christ.

And each time the man told the young usher, 'I can pray right here where I'm sitting, young man. I don't need to go forward to pray or become a Christian!' And this usher always responded courteously, 'I'm sorry, sir, but you are wrong. You cannot pray here. You must go forward if you want to make a commitment to accept Jesus Christ as your Lord and Saviour'. This conversation was repeated almost verbatim every night, but the business man was determined not to respond with a show of 'public emotion', as he called it.

But then came the last night in the series of meetings. The distinguished-looking man took the same seat he had occupied each night previously. The evangelist preached and for the last time he invited people in the audience to respond, by coming to the front of the auditorium, to indicate their desire to give their lives to Jesus Christ. Once more the usher invited the man to go to the front. 'I'll go with you, sir,' he said, 'if you want to go to the front to give your life to Christ.'

This time the man looked up with tears in his eyes. He had been deeply touched by the preaching. He replied to the young man, 'Oh, would you please go with me. I need to give my life to Christ. I'm ready to go forward and pray'. To which the usher replied, 'Sir, you don't need to go forward to accept the Lord. You can pray right here where you are sitting!'

When this distinguished man was ready to humble himself, then the Lord could respond to him where he was. The lost son finally came to the same attitude. He acknowledged his guilt. It was then that the change took place in his heart. His father was wanting him to reach this attitude of brokenness and sorrow for his sin. The father longed earnestly to have an unbroken heart relationship with his wayward son, but he knew that was not possible unless his son had a change of heart. Every day his father stood at the end of the road and watched for him. How he longed for him to return. How great was his patience and compassion.

The son could not blame his father for his problems. He ended up eating with pigs because of his own foolishness. When he realized how foolish he had been, he repented of his selfishness, and decided to return home to his waiting father. In this story, grace and repentance meet each other. Because he knew his father was so loving, the son decided to return home, acknowledging his wrong attitude and actions. It was the knowledge of his father's love that finally brought him to the place of repentance. I believe that to know the Father is to love him! And to love the Father is to return to him.

Our heavenly Father longs for us to return 'home'. Whatever your problem, whatever your need, the Father is waiting for you to return to him. The Bible says that 'the Lord waits to be gracious to you; therefore he exalts himself to show mercy to you' (Is 30:18). In another place it says, 'Do you not know that God's kindness is meant to lead you to repentance?' (Rom 2:4).

He is the waiting Father.

He loved his son so much that when he did return home he did not condemn his son for his wrong actions, but forgave him and celebrated his return with a great feast! What a great father! In fact, as we read this parable again, we notice that he is not just a waiting father! He is the running father. When he sees his dirty, weary, guilty son coming down the road, hesitant and uncertain about his father's response to him, he runs to him and puts his arms around him and embraces him.

There is no reserve in his heart towards this one who has sinned. He is totally forgiving. His joy says it all.

See what manner of love the Father has given to us! He calls us 'son', or 'daughter'. We are princes and princesses. We belong to the King. He is our Father! He does not force us to be his. It is our choice and when we do rebel and act selfishly, he doesn't grow cold and hard, and ignore us. He weeps over us and waits for us. Every day he looks for us, anxiously awaiting our return. And when we come back he celebrates our return with a great, joyful banquet.

He does not condone our rebellion or selfishness. It grieves him deeply to see us hurting ourselves and others. It is wrong and we know it, for he has told us often. It is his grief, his broken heart, his compassion, his willingness to give so much love that finally wins our hearts. To know him is to love him. And to love him is to obey him.

And we should not think that because he is so forgiving his love is sentimental or soft. He is strong. He can roar like a lion. There is great strength in his quietness – no one who knows him can doubt that. He is no hollow God. His ruthless hatred of evil tolerates no double-mindedness, but his compassion is endless towards those who see their need of him. He sees our hearts. He knows our innermost thoughts. There is great security beneath the gaze of those pure, piercing eyes for all those who sincerely want to be in his family.

The Bible describes the character of our waiting Father in many ways. It leaves no room to blame him for any injustice. Though many blame him for their problems and their hurts, it is clear that his character is without blemish. Consider just some of these qualities the Bible teaches about God.

1. Creator

One who creates us in his image, with freedom to choose whether to respond to his love.

'In him we live and move and have our being . . . for we are indeed his offspring' (Acts 17:28).

'Oh Lord, thou art our Father; we are the clay, and thou art our potter; we are all the work of thy hand' (Is 64:8).

2. Provider

One who loves to provide for our physical, emotional, mental and spiritual needs.

'If you then, who are evil, know how to give good gifts to your children, how much more will your Father who is in heaven give good gifts to those who ask him!' (Mt 7:11).

3. Friend and counsellor

One who longs to have intimate friendship with us and to share wise counsel and instruction with us.

'Thou art the friend of my youth' (Jer 3:4).

'And his name will be called Wonderful Counsellor, Mighty God, Everlasting Father, Prince of Peace' (Is 9:6).

'Thou dost guide me with thy counsel' (Ps 73:24).

4. Corrector

One who lovingly corrects and disciplines us.

'My son, do not regard lightly the discipline of the Lord . . . for the Lord disciplines him whom he loves, and chastises every son whom he receives . . . . If you are left without discipline . . . then you are illegitimate children and not sons. For the moment all discipline seems painful rather than pleasant; later it yields the peaceful fruit of righteousness to those who have been trained by it' (Heb 12:5–6,8,11).

5. Redeemer

One who forgives his children's faults and brings good out of their failures and weaknesses; one who brings us back from being lost.

'The Lord is merciful and gracious, slow to anger and abounding in steadfast love. As far as the east is from the west, so far does he remove our transgressions from us. As a father pities his children, so the Lord pities those who fear him' (Ps 103:8,12–13).

6. Comforter

One who cares for us and comforts us in times of need.

'Blessed be the God and Father of our Lord Jesus Christ, the Father of mercies and God of all comfort, who comforts us in all our affliction' (2 Cor 1:3).

7. Defender and deliverer

One who loves to protect, defend and deliver his children.

'He who dwells in the shelter of the Most High, who abides in the shadow of the Almighty, will say to the Lord, "My refuge and my fortress; my God, in whom I trust". For he will deliver you . . .' (Ps 91:1–3).

8. Father

One who wants to free us from all false gods so that he can be a Father to us.

'And I will be a father to you, and you shall be my sons and daughters says the Lord Almighty' (2 Cor 6:18).

9. Father of the fatherless

One who cares for the homeless and the widow.

'Father of the fatherless and protector of widows is God in his holy habitation. God gives the desolate a home to dwell in' (Ps 68:5–6).

10. Father of love

One who reveals himself to us and reconciles us to himself through Jesus Christ.

'For the Father himself loves you, because you have loved me and have believed that I came from the Father' (Jn 16:27).

There are many other terms in the Bible used to describe the character of our Father God. Listed below are a few of those terms and Scripture references you may want to refer to, as you meditate on the character of our wonderful God. He is:

Patient	Ps 78:35–39
Considerate	Jn 2:1–11; 19:25–27
Holy	Jn 2:13–22
Discerning	Jn 2:23–25
Compassionate	Lk 19:1–10
Sensitive	Lk 8:40–48
Caring	Mt 9:35–38
Tender	Jn 12:1–8
Gracious	Jn 4:7–27
Forgiving	Jn 8:1–11
Just	Deut 32:4–5
Loving and Kind	Ex 34:6–7
Merciful	Lam 3:23; Lk 23:29–43
Thoughtful	Lk 18:15–17
Generous	Mt 14:13–21; 15:30–38
Powerful	Mt 17:14–21
Wise	Mt 17:24–27
Mighty	Mk 4:35–41
Loving	Lk 6:27–36

Despite all that the Bible teaches about God as loving and just, there was a time in my life when I respected him, but I did not love him. I even feared him, because of his awesome power, but I did not love him for his goodness.

It was when I looked beyond my ideas about God, beyond my desire to argue and discuss, and asked God to reveal to me how he saw my selfishness, that I began to experience a deeper relationship with God.

It was then that I discovered the broken heart of God.

3
Why God Heals Wounded Hearts

François took the French government to court to force them to stop giving him money! Sounds incredible, doesn't it? His story is one of the most unusual I have ever encountered, and illustrates the great love and power of God to heal and transform a person's life.

He came to us several years ago when Sally and I lived on the 'Ark' in Amsterdam. (The Ark is a Christian community, a kind of half-way house, that takes in people suffering from life controlling problems. It was situated at that time on two large houseboats that sat in the harbour behind the Central Train Station.) When I first saw François, his eyes were unfocused and vacant, and his hair was long, curly and unkempt. He spoke very little English. After several hours, two of our French-speaking workers were able to decipher his situation. He was using LSD and morphine regularly, and he had been involved in a car accident which had rendered him permanently disabled due to brain damage. He was also in a state of drug-induced psychosis (which meant that he was totally out of touch with reality due to his use of psychedelic drugs). We had found him standing at the end of the pier next to our boats, contemplating suicide. He had lost the desire to live and his ability to cope with reality as he knew it.

And no wonder: brain damage, family rejection, drugs, occult bondage, psychological problems – life offered no hope. The French government declared him incapacitated for life and gave him a monthly pension.

After ten months of prayer and fasting and many hundreds of hours of counselling and care, one of the young men who had committed himself to help François came to me and said, 'François wants to talk to you. He doesn't feel he should continue to receive the monthly pension the French government is giving him.'

'Why not?' I asked, a bit astounded at this latest turn of events.

'I think it is best if François explains it to you himself.'

The ensuing conversation has to be one of the most rewarding in the twenty or so years I have spent helping people out with their problems. In broken English, learned in the ten months he had lived with us on the Ark, François demonstrated to me just how deep the healing was that had taken place in his life.

He was thinking clearly, and not just about himself. He displayed Christian compassion and a desire to be a responsible person. How different this conversation was to the one I had had with him months earlier when he first came to the Ark! In those ten months, François had experienced freedom from occult bondage, and profound psychological and physical healing. This doesn't mean he was without problems or that he had worked through all the accumulated wounds of the past, but the healing he had experienced was real and, as the last eleven years have proved, it was permanent. During those ten months, François had come to the conclusion that life had meaning for him personally. He no longer wanted to die. In fact, he had developed a testy sort of stubbornness about life and what he wanted to do. He felt very definitely that he was to tell others about the forgiveness of sin, and wholeness of personality that he had found through putting his trust in Jesus Christ. He wanted to be an evangelist!

But first there was the little problem of the French government to deal with. François returned to France to tell the authorities he was not 'crazy', and that he could work as a responsible citizen to provide for himself. The authorities had never had anyone ask *not* to receive disability compensation. They felt sure he *must* be crazy!

So, they *refused* to stop sending François the monthly payments. But that did not deter him. After praying and seeking counsel from others, he decided to find a lawyer and take the French government to court, to force them to stop the disability compensation. Little did he imagine the surprises that were in store for him.

Some 'friends' of François contacted his lawyer and convinced him that it was in the 'best interest of all' that François should continue to receive his pension, and that he should testify against François in the trial. Much to François' surprise he did this. He was crestfallen. It was the last day of the hearing when things changed.

The judge called François to the bench to question him one more time.

'You say you are a Christian, young man?'

'Yes, sir.'

'And you believe that Jesus Christ has changed your life?' asked the judge.

'Yes, sir.'

'And you also believe he has healed you of your past problems, and you can work now?'

'Yes, sir.'

One more time the judge repeated the question, 'You believe in Jesus Christ as your personal Saviour, and that he has forgiven you of your sins?'

'Yes, sir.'

'Very good, young man. So do I! Case dismissed.'

The judge decided in favour of François. He too believed in Jesus Christ as his personal Saviour! Against unbelievable odds, particularly in France, God had seen to it that a Christian judge heard François' case. François was overjoyed. In spite of his past problems, and in spite of the efforts of disloyal friends and his own lawyer testifying against him, God had given him a victory. As a young Christian, François had seen God at work on his behalf as he did what was right.

This does not mean from that moment onwards François had no more problems. Although God does perform miracles of healing and restoration, he normally does this through a process, rather than instantaneously. God wants to involve us in the healing process. We must respond to God's love in obedience and humility for the healing to take place. This process is called 'sanctification'. (Sanctification means to make something clean that was dirty, in the sense of evil or selfishness; it also means to be set apart to be made pure or holy, to be made whole.)

It is very encouraging to see that the Bible speaks specifically about healing for damaged emotions. In the Old Testament book of Isaiah, the writer points to the future when God will send a Saviour to rescue people from their sin and selfishness. Isaiah 53:3 says that the

Saviour will be 'a man of sorrows, and acquainted with grief'. It goes on to say that 'he has borne our griefs and carried our sorrows', and that 'with his stripes we are healed'. This healing is for both the guilt of our selfishness and the *consequences* of selfishness – the scars and wounds we bear in our personalities and emotions. In chapter 6 of the same book we are told that the Messiah, the Saviour, will 'bring good tidings to the afflicted . . . bind up the brokenhearted . . . proclaim liberty to the captives, and the opening of the prison to those who are bound'; and it says that those of us who mourn will be given the 'oil of gladness'. In Psalm 34:18 David says that 'The Lord is near to the brokenhearted, and saves the crushed in spirit'. The psalmist says in chapter 147:3 that the Lord 'heals the brokenhearted, and binds up their wounds'. *This is good news for a broken world.*

In spite of what Jesus has done for us, some people still wonder why God sits up in heaven, removed from the pain and harsh reality of this fallen world. They feel betrayed by God and they are bitter towards him because of that. 'Why has he created us and then abandoned us?' they question.

After being caught between two friends involved in a very hurtful disagreement, which brought to the surface some old wounds, one friend of mine found himself out in a field one night crying out to God, saying, 'I forgive you, I forgive you, I forgive you.' Until that point he had not realized that he had, quite mistakenly, been holding God responsible for what happened. In a way he was blaming God for the difficulties his friends were experiencing.

Don't many of us do the same thing? In our heart of hearts we often hold God responsible for the hurtful things people do to us, secretly nurturing the hidden feeling that, in the final analysis, he is to blame.

But God is not to blame. He is not the author of evil, nor does he tempt us with evil. He is just in all his ways, and kind in all he does. He is not the cause of our problems and he has not abandoned us in the midst of our problems. God came and lived among us. He became a man. He suffered all that we have gone through and much more.

God created man and man rejected him. God sent messengers and prophets to remind man that it was he who had created him but they stoned the prophets and killed the messengers. So finally God came himself. The Creator stepped into his creation, but the creatures refused to recognize their maker. In fact, the creatures crucified the Creator on a cross. What did the Creator do then? He turned this, the greatest of mankind's cruelties, around and made it the source of man's forgiveness! *We killed him and he used the act of our greatest selfishness to be the source of our forgiveness.*

Jesus Christ is the wounded healer. He has gone through all the pain and suffering that mankind has ever experienced. The Bible says that he was tempted in every way that we have been tempted. Speaking of Jesus, as a priest for us, the Bible says: 'We have not a high priest who is unable to sympathize with our weaknesses, but one who in every respect has been tempted as we are, yet without sinning. Let us then with confidence draw near to the throne of grace, that we may receive mercy and find grace to help in time of need' (Heb 4:15–16).

Do you hear what this is really saying? Do you see how different Jesus is from all those who have served in his name, but who have not cared for those they served? Jesus is in a class by himself. He is God, but a God we can come to freely, and a God who is not afraid to be involved with us. In fact, he has gone through what we have gone through so we would know for sure that he really loves us. He sat alone, abandoned by all his friends. He faced prejudice and deep rejection. He knew what it is to lose his father. He did not stay up in his holy heaven, far removed from the reality of this world. He came as one of us.

He was born into poverty. His race was ostracized and his home town ridiculed. He was not good-looking, and people questioned his friendships. His father died when he was young. In his latter years he travelled the streets and cities homeless. He was misunderstood in his ministry, and abandoned in death. He did all this for you and me. He did it to identify with us in weakness. But he also did it as a sacrificial act of suffering in our place, in order that we might be whole.

Jesus Christ, God's Son, came into the world to bring us healing and hope. We live in alienation because of our selfishness, and the selfishness of those who have sinned against us. We experience this alienation within ourselves, with God and with others. Jesus came to introduce reconciliation in place of alienation, healing in place of wounds, and wholeness in place of personality fragmentation.

The Bible also teaches that Jesus Christ is coming again. When he comes for the second time, he will culminate the healing and reconciliation process that he began for all mankind when he first came two thousand years ago. He will finish what he started. We can look forward to his second coming, because of the reality of his first coming. He will do away with suffering and sorrow, with sickness and disease, and with all selfishness. Then he will rule the earth with awesome power. But *now* he rules with patience and mercy. He has come to establish his rule, but he wishes to win men's hearts with love, not with force or might.

'His kingdom', that is, his rule in men's hearts, has come, but it is not fully here. The Bible promises that when he fully establishes his rule, all sickness, suffering and emotional pain will be done away with. We have begun to see those things now, but they will be fully realized when he returns again. They are substantial even now, but they will be complete then.

Why has he done it this way? Why hasn't he fully established his rule with all those promises fully realized *right now*? It is because he is seeking to establish his authority through our voluntary responses. He could use armies and absolute power to force men to serve him, but what good is it if we serve him out of fear, not love? That's not what he wants. He could use miracles and money to seduce us, but what good is it if we only serve him because of what we get from him, and not because we love him for who he is?

He is seeking to find the people that will fulfil his original intentions when he created mankind. *He wants friendship from us.* And he does not just want this with a collection of selfish individuals. His purpose is to unite all those who love him into a family. So whenever people love him he draws them together to enjoy deep friendship, mutual care and support, and celebration of the love, forgiveness and wholeness that he has given them. These family units are what the church is intended to be.

The 'Father's family' is also a channel of his love and healing to wounded people. As we love, accept and forgive one another, as God's children and as brothers and sisters, God's love flows through us to heal one another. Fellowship and friendship are one of the sacraments of the church. A sacrament has been traditionally defined as a means of grace. The

WHY GOD HEALS WOUNDED HEARTS

sacraments include such things as baptism in water and the Lord's Supper. Through our brothers and sisters in God's family, God provides the kind of love and acceptance that frees us from our fears and allows us to grow into greater wholeness as people. We can be ourselves, and be committed to others without fear of rejection. We can accept others in spite of their weaknesses. We can forgive even when others hurt us. All of this is because of God's grace. It is his grace, that is his undeserved love, that does this for us. We don't have the ability within ourselves to be so loving. But God enables us to love that way. We don't have the ability within ourselves to heal one another, but through us God heals others. Every Christian has this ministry. We are 'grace givers'.

At this point it is important to bring a gentle warning. If we are wounded, we should be careful not to put our focus on people as the *source* of healing in our lives. People cannot give what only God can give. *If you want people to heal you, you will easily be disappointed.* Focus your attention on the heavenly Father, he is the only one capable of healing you totally. He will often do that *through* people, but remember that he is the source and people are the channel.

Emotional healing is almost always a process. It takes time. There is a very important reason for this. Our heavenly Father is not only wanting to free us from the pain of past wounds, he is also desirous of bringing us into maturity, both spiritually and emotionally. That takes time, because we need time to learn to make right choices. He loves us enough to take the months and years necessary to not only heal our wounds, but also build our character. Without growth of character we will get wounded again. We will do foolish, selfish things that will hurt us or provoke others to hurt us.

Because he loves us he waits for us to want this kind of character growth. He waits for us to be ready to be healed. Often it is our right response to others that releases this healing into our lives.

How God heals wounded hearts

In the next chapter I have listed the steps involved in the healing of emotional and psychological wounds. I have not intended these steps to be treated as some sort of magic formula or talisman to wave in God's face. The truths that each one of these steps represent must be applied to our hearts as we are ready for them and with the guidance of God's Spirit. (If you don't know how to be guided by God's Spirit, ask him to help you. He has promised to help all those who ask him.) Take each step and apply it personally to your situation.

If your problems are complex you may need the help of a professional counsellor or psychiatrist. In the back of this book is an appendix with guidelines on how to choose a professional counsellor or psychiatrist. You have a right to ask them questions before you allow them to ask you questions. I think it is very important to stress that you should never submit yourself to being helped or counselled by someone, unless you feel very secure with them, and *very* confident that they are skilled and competent enough to help you. There is a world of difference between a Christian friend who tries to help you through encouragement and love, and someone who professes to be a 'counsellor', but is not qualified.

We don't have to live with pain. Because of God's love for us and because Jesus has suffered in our place, we don't have to carry our wounds with us all our lives. We can be healed and set free.

4
How God Heals Wounded Hearts

I once met a man who said he had never sinned! It was in an open market-place in Madras, India. Because of our mutual interest in religion, our casual conversation quickly turned serious. When I shared that I believed God was basically forgiving to those who acknowledged their sinfulness, he asserted that he had never once done anything wrong in his entire life!

'You've never lied?' I asked him.

'No, never,' came the answer.

'You mean you've never stolen something or hated someone?'

'No, not ever once.'

'Have you committed adultery?'

'No.'

'Disobeyed your parents?'

'No.'

'Cheated in an exam at school?'

'No, not that either.'

I was baffled. Then I thought of another question. 'I bet you are proud of the fact that you have never sinned, aren't you?' I asked mischievously.

'Oh yes,' he replied, 'very proud, very proud!'

'There you are,' I said, 'you've just sinned for the first time! You are a proud man!' To which he laughed loudly and congratulated me that I had caught him in his only sin!

Though we are not all as proud as this man was, we have all ratified Adam's original sin. Adam denied God's right to rule over his life and chose to go his own way – and we have all done the same thing. It is hard for us to admit that we too have rebelled against God and denied his right to be God in our lives.

Without acknowledging this, the most basic of all mankind's problems (our selfishness), dealing with the wounds and unmet needs in our lives only postpones the inevitable. Pain-killers cannot keep a terminally ill cancer patient alive. They may take the pain away, and that is important when one is in pain, but why take the pain-killer if there is a permanent cure for the cancer?

So it is with us, if we seek emotional pain-killers, but deny our most basic problem. Wonderfully, God longs to forgive us if we will only acknowledge our pride and selfishness and ask him to forgive us. Our deep, inner reactions to doing this should only confirm the truth of our need to do so.

By telling us that we have rebelled against him, God is not saying he condemns us or rejects us. Some people feel that God is rejecting them when they read in the Bible that they are sinners. That is not the case at all. God is simply helping us to understand the most basic problem we have and how to overcome it.

But we are not only sinners. We are also *sinned against*. There are things done to us, against us, by others, either intentionally through their selfishness or unintentionally simply because they are not perfect, that deeply affect us. Being sinned against, does not excuse wrong responses on our part, but it helps us to understand ourselves, and others, as we struggle to respond in the right way when we have been mistreated or hurt.

To gain the maximum healing and blessing, I suggest you go through the following steps slowly and prayerfully. Take time after reading each step to pray and apply it to your life. If it becomes painful ask a friend, or spiritual leader or someone he refers you to, to go through the steps with you. You need to be prepared for some pain if there are unhealed wounds. In order for them to heal properly, old wounds may need to be opened and cleansed of any 'infection', or bitterness that has set in. Even though it may be painful for a time, it will bring great joy and healing in the long run. Don't try to run away from facing your problems or you will only postpone the time when you need 'surgery'.

How God heals our wounds

Step 1: Acknowledge your need of healing

For most people this doesn't present a problem. But if we are wounded and do not acknowledge that we have a need, there is obviously no room for healing or help in our lives. To acknowledge our need is a sign of good mental health, as well as just being plain-old honest!

All of us need healing and growth in our emotions and personality. *Don't feel that you are an exception.* It is willingness to learn and humility that will allow God to work in your life. Some of us struggle with admitting our need, for fear of rejection. But the opposite is really true. When we admit our needs, others respect us more for our honesty. We can all recall a time when we made ourselves vulnerable and shared our needs, and then someone did not respond to us in love or wisdom. But don't let that experience keep you from the healing God wants to give you. Rise above the smallness of other people's actions. Don't let past rejection determine your actions or attitudes for the future.

Start by being honest with God. He knows everything anyway. He won't reject you. In fact, he is longing and waiting for you to be honest, so you can receive his love and help. Share everything with him. Tell him your hurts, fears, disappointments – *everything*. He loves honesty.

Then you need to open up to someone who can help you work through these steps of healing.

If you have wronged others you will need to go to them as well, and make it right. This is all part of acknowledging your needs. You do this not in order to be forgiven by God, but because you have been forgiven. The fruit of being in the right relationship with God is wanting to have broken relationships with others restored as well.

John Stott gives some very valuable cautions in this area in his book *Confess Your Sins*. He talks about the circle of confession: secret sins, private sins and public sins. We should only confess sins on the level they occurred. If it was a secret sin, that is, a sin of the heart or mind that was never acted or spoken out to others, then it only needs to be confessed to God. There is freedom of course to share these things with close friends or fellow Christians, out of a desire to be honest and to be accountable in areas of weakness in our lives, but we don't have to do that. That is our choice. In fact, we should only do it when we feel secure with others, and when we feel God is specifically leading us to do so, and never because we feel pressured to do so. Even then we must be wise and careful about how we share.

It could be very unwise to confess some sins of the heart to others. If it is our sin, and if the person we sinned against in our mind doesn't know it, we should not burden them with this sin, unless there is a clear reason why it will be helpful to them. If in doubt, mature counsel should be sought first.

There are some sins that are committed on the secret or private level of our lives that are shameful in nature. I believe we need to see a restoration of a sense of shame – particularly over sins of sexual impurity.

If you are in a meeting where *God* is leading people to confess their sins publicly, you should not feel pressure to confess publicly those things you have done in private. If you feel God wants you to say something, you can obey the Lord and at the same time be wise by simply saying, 'I have failed the Lord,' or, 'God has shown me how great his forgiveness is in spite of my past disobedience,' or, 'I have not lived up to the light I have had and God is showing me I have been a hypocrite. He wants me to confess that I have failed him, and I receive his forgiveness'.

Do not confess sexual sins in public under pressure from other people. If for no other reason it is unwise because you could present other people with temptations of unclean thoughts or burden them with impure pictures in their minds. People sitting in a group should not be burdened with confessions of someone's sexual sins without being asked if they want to hear such things. The very act of doing this can bring disgrace to the Lord, advertise sin, put pressure on others to feel that they too have to dig up their past sins and confess them. It may even lead people to confess things publicly that have not been put right with other individuals involved in the situation. At times it is helpful to share these things with a mature counsellor if we are struggling with condemnation and a feeling that God cannot forgive us, but we should not do that publicly.

If you must ask an individual to forgive you for sinning against them in this way, do not go into details or be unwise in your words. Say only what needs to be said. Confess that you have failed them or sinned against them and ask their forgiveness. That is enough.

A good rule of thumb to follow is if it is a secret sin, confess it to God; if it is a private sin, ask forgiveness of the one you have sinned against; and if it is a public sin, ask the group's forgiveness.

If you are weak in a particular area, it could be very helpful to share that with a few respected friends for the sake of accountability, but again, you should do it out of a sense of security and safety with these people and not because you feel pressured to do so.

To summarize, the steps to healing and wholeness, as related to honesty about our needs, go something like this:

(1) Be honest about needs and sins. Honesty about our needs or sins releases God's grace in our lives.

(2) Receive God's grace. Grace is God's gift of love, acceptance and forgiveness to us, and it makes us secure in him. That security releases faith in God in our hearts.

(3) Trust the Lord and others. Faith releases trust and makes it possible for us to have heart relationships with God and others.

(4) Build heart relationships with God and others. Relationships of love and trust with God and others are made possible because we have

humbled ourselves. God can then release love
and forgiveness both to us and in our hearts
towards others.

The opposite of this process is also possible:
   (1) Broken relationships. When relationships are
       broken we find it very difficult to trust others.
   (2) Legalistic. When our relationship with others
       is wrong, we tend to become judgemental and
       critical. We live by 'law' not grace. This causes
       us to mistrust others.
   (3) Mistrust. When we don't trust others we often
       project our mistrust which results in our
       feeling that others don't trust us. An
       atmosphere of rejection grows and walls come
       between us and others.
   (4) Walls. Walls produce separation, the very
       opposite of heart relationships.

In looking at being honest about our needs, it is
important to distinguish between a sin, a wound and a
bondage. For sin there needs to be forgiveness, for a
wound there needs to be healing, and for spiritual
bondage we need to be set free. Sometimes we need
help in all three areas. You cannot confess a wound as
if it were a sin because a wound is not a sin. But if as a
result of being hurt you have developed a sinful attitude
or response, even if others are to blame, *God still holds
you responsible for your response*. In fact, God does
not see it as a matter of the other person being 80% to
blame and you 20%, but both you and the other person
are 100% responsible for your actions. Until you accept
100% responsibility for your actions, healing is blocked
in your life. Why is that? If your attitude is one of
resentment, bitterness, or an unforgiving attitude,
God's healing and forgiveness are blocked. 'For if you
forgive men their trespasses, your heavenly Father also

will forgive you; but if you do not forgive men their trespasses, neither will your Father forgive your trespasses' (Mt 6:14–15).

To summarize this point, I cannot overstress the importance of acknowledging our need of healing if it is there in our lives. I have seen many people busy doing things for God, but their activity has been tainted by their need to prove themselves, or to gain acceptance, or by insecurity about what they were doing. Our service to God and to other people should flow out of our security and sense of well being, not out of a drive to prove ourselves or a need to 'be somebody'. In the long run we will please God, we will feel much better about ourselves, we will enjoy our work much more and we will be a greater blessing to others, if we take time to grow into wholeness and emotional healing.

Step 2: Confessing negative emotions

Some of us go through life collecting negative emotions. We were not taught by example how to identify or how to communicate our feelings, so we have stored negative feelings such as anger, disappointment, fear, bitterness and guilt since early childhood. Emotions that are not spoken out can be stored up inside us. Suppressing one emotion on top of another is like pushing one layer after another of rubbish into a plastic rubbish bag: something finally has to give. This process of building up unidentified and uncommunicated emotions produces terrible side effects. Everything from ulcers to suicide can result: we don't learn how to cope with difficulties, we grow up physically while our emotional development is retarded, and there is a great block to giving and receiving in our relationships with others and with God. Some of the major emotions that we often build up include rejection, anger, fear and guilt.

Dr Phil Blakely, a Christian psychologist, notes that to deal with this problem we need to 'decompact,' that is, to talk out the emotions built up inside us. To do this it is important to have someone to help us get our feelings out. For Christians, that should begin in prayer. If Jesus is not the one we turn to, before all others and above all others, we will never be healed. He is our Creator and our heavenly Father. He longs for us to share our feelings with him because he cares so deeply for us.

Of course, we need to talk to others as well. It is important to develop friendships with people who allow us to be ourselves, but who love us enough to challenge us when we are wrong.

Compacted emotions are not the root cause of our problems, but they can be a serious hindrance to recognizing and dealing with the root causes, and they can become a major problem in themselves if they are compacted internally over a long period of time. Of course communicating our emotions is not a panacea in itself. Communication of our feelings clears the channels so the root causes can be dealt with. If we communicate stored up feelings of guilt, that does not mean we have dealt with the causes of the guilt. This is where there is a major breakdown in relativistic psychology. To get people talking about their guilt feelings can make them feel better, but in the long run if one does not accept responsibility for violating God's moral laws, the feelings of guilt will return (unless of course a person completely sears his conscience and loses the ability to feel at all). Though emotions in themselves are not sinful, they can result in sinful attitudes if they are directed in a negative way towards God, ourselves, or others. That is where we need God's standards, as taught in the Bible, to be the measure for judging whether or not our emotions have become sinful. If they have become sinful we must treat them as both *unhealthy* and *wrong*.

God does not intend us to live by our feelings or for our feelings. Some people live by the axiom that if they feel good after something it is good, and if they feel bad, it is bad. That may be good existentialism, but it is not biblical Christianity. Truth as revealed to us in the Bible is to guide our lives, not feelings. God has given us the capacity for emotions and he intended them to be an encouragement for making right choices. If we do not live by God's laws, then we will twist his original intentions for emotions, and use them to reinforce a lifestyle of pleasure and selfishness. God did not give us the ability to experience emotions (feelings) so they would rule over us, but he gave them to us as servants for more godly living. Some people are totally ruled by their emotions, while others don't even know they have deeper feelings. They have suppressed their feelings to the point where they think it is very 'Christian' not to show any emotions at all. This is not being mature or 'spiritual'. God created us to live a balanced life where we express and enjoy our emotions, and where we are free to deal with them honestly and constructively, but he did not create us to be prisoners of our emotions.

Husbands, fathers, and spiritual leaders can be a great help to those they know, if they allow them the opportunity to share their feelings freely. Our desire to lead others can be ineffective or even harmful if those we lead are not given that opportunity. By creating room for those around us to be honest, we can lead them into a deeper relationship with God. Those we lead will trust us more and will sense our commitment to them, which in turn gives us the freedom to speak into their lives. Where there is no trust we have no authority. By giving people the opportunity to be honest we are 'giving grace', which in turn gives us the security to be honest about not only their emotions, but also the needs they have in their life.

If those we are leading have a serious mistrust of others, especially authority figures, it could be that they have never learned to express their feelings honestly in an atmosphere of love and acceptance.

My wife, Sally, once shared with me some personal problems she was experiencing. My response was to begin to give her advice on how to get out of the problem. I'll never forget her response to me. 'I didn't come to you so that you could exhort me or preach to me,' she said. 'I know what I need to do. When you exhort me it makes me feel as if you're not listening or caring. *I need someone to listen to me. If I can't talk to you, who can I go to?*'

I decided right then that I wanted to be the kind of husband who gave the freedom and security to my wife – and to others for that matter – to share their feelings with me without fear of judgement, sermonizing or reprisal. Of course I have also had to help others learn how to do that in such a way so that they are not negative or demanding.

To break this cycle of emotional suppression and mistrust, ask God to give you the opportunity to share with a figure of authority that gives you the freedom to be honest about your feelings. (And, of course, you must forgive those in the past who have not given you that freedom.) Your motive in sharing how you feel should not be to persuade others of your point of view, but to be honest.

However, honesty is not an end in itself. It is possible to be ruthlessly honest and at the same time be very cruel.

If someone tells you all your faults in a cold, uncaring manner, totally unconcerned about the effect of their words on you, then their honesty is not virtuous but exactly the opposite: it is an expression of their great lack of love. And it is also possible for a sinner to be 'honest' about his sins but to show no remorse at all for his wrong-doing. The motive for being honest should be to become the person God wants you to be, not just the opportunity to vent your feelings or have a few nice relationships.

If we have been hurt by an authority figure or disagree with them, it is our responsibility to seek God first before we go to them. If we don't understand a decision they have made by praying about it, then we can ask them to clarify their point of view. We can feel free to disagree with a leader, but we shouldn't allow that to affect our attitude. We can disagree without becoming judgemental or breaking fellowship. Disunity never takes place because of disagreement. It is because we go beyond disagreeing to criticizing or judging someone. *There is no problem of unity that cannot be solved with greater humility or forgiveness.* God is concerned about our attitude of heart, as well as helping us grow by being open and honest about our feelings.

To summarize, it is important to communicate suppressed emotions. Keeping them inside can be very unhealthy, as well as leading to bad attitudes. But in getting them out, God wants us to accept responsibility for how we share our feelings and how we allow our feelings to affect our words, actions and attitudes. Honesty, together with responsibility for our actions, makes it possible to receive God's healing when we are suffering from emotional pain.

Step 3: Forgive those who have hurt you

Forgiveness is not forgetting a wrong that someone has

committed against us, nor is it a mystical kind of spiritual feeling. It is simply pardoning the person for the wrong they have done. It is showing love and acceptance in spite of being hurt.

Forgiveness is often a process and not a once-only act. We keep on forgiving until the pain goes away. The deeper the wound the greater the forgiveness needed. Just as a doctor has to keep a physical wound in our bodies clean from infection so the wound can heal properly, so we must keep our emotional wounds clean of bitterness so they can heal. Forgiveness keeps the wounds clean. Whenever you think of a particular person and feel hurt, forgive them. It is not complicated. Just tell the Lord that you forgive that person, and that you choose to love them with God's love. Receive his love for them by faith. Keep doing that every time you think of the person, until you feel God's love released in your heart for them.

The motivation to exercise that forgiveness is God's forgiveness for us. If you find it difficult to forgive someone else, just think for a while about how much God has forgiven *you*. If it does not seem like a lot then you need to go further and ask God for a revelation of your heart as he sees it. Ask him to show the hardness of your heart. Ask God to do anything he needs, to break up the hard ground of your heart until it becomes soft with compassion. God will answer your prayer if you cry out to him sincerely and desperately.

Step 4: Receive forgiveness

If you have been hurt by others and have sinned in your reaction to them, it is important to not only forgive the ones who hurt you, but also to ask God for forgiveness for your wrong actions towards them. As you do this, you may discover a need to forgive yourself. At times our greatest enemy is our own sense of failure. We can often be much harder on ourselves than anyone else.

If you have failed, confess your sin to the Lord and then tell him that you receive his forgiveness and that you forgive yourself. Each time you feel that sense of failure returning, tell the Lord you do not receive it because he has forgiven you.

There is a difference between conviction of sin and condemnation. Condemnation is from a sense of failure. Conviction is because we have sinned. Conviction is specific and clear and from God; condemnation is vague and general and from ourselves or the enemy, Satan.

If you think you have sinned, but are not sure, ask God for conviction. If it does not come as you wait before him in prayer, thank him for his love and forgiveness and go on with your day. Remain open to him showing you any wrong attitude, but do not become paralysed by introspection. If God wants to show you any wrong attitudes, he is capable of doing so if you remain open to him. Do not wallow in the pigsty of self-pity. It is too destructive.

If you have wrong attitudes towards anyone who has hurt you, it is crucial that you confess this to God. But be careful: self-pity can be a counterfeit for real repentance. Dealing with our part in the matter often releases God's Spirit to work in the hearts of others. Even if this does not happen it is still our responsibility to keep our hearts right before God. If we become critical, hard-hearted, jealous, independent, proud, judgemental, unbroken in our heart attitude or bitter, *then we need to deal with our responses*. As we are broken before God then he will forgive us and heal our wounds.

There is healing through forgiveness!

Step 5: Receive the Father's love

There is a void in our lives that can only be filled by God himself. When you sin and ask for forgiveness, or you struggle with insecurity or inferiority, there is the possibility that that void is not full. Ask God at those times to fill you with his Spirit. Stand against self-consciousness with God-centredness. I cannot overstress the importance of this step in the healing process. *Self-pity and self-centredness grieve the Holy Spirit.* If you have grieved the Spirit of God, then you are not filled with his Spirit. Ask him to forgive you whenever you grieve him, and to fill you with his Holy Spirit. Receive the Spirit by faith (Eph 4:25–5:21).

As you do this, focus your thoughts and prayers on his character and on different aspects of his father heart. Worship him, that is, speak to him, sing to him, and think on him; concentrate on his faithfulness, his holiness, his purity, his compassion, his mercy, his forgiveness and his unchangeableness.

Developing an attitude of worship is one of the greatest keys I know to receiving the Father's love. Cultivate this trait above all others. Memorize scriptures or songs that you can use as weapons to combat loneliness or discouragement. Worship is the doorway that leads into the Father's presence. Worship is the pathway that leads you away from depression and self-pity. Some people say they cannot worship God when they don't feel like it because that would be hypocritical. My answer to that is that we don't worship God because of how we feel, but because of *who he is*. I often worship God *in spite of my feelings*. I don't want to be a prisoner of my feelings, so I praise God anyway.

I try to be honest with God about how I'm feeling, but then I start to focus on who he is and not on how I feel.

Do you want to receive the Father's love? Then spend time in his presence. Receiving his love is not like receiving a piece of something; it is the result of being with God. We are bathed in his love as we spend time in his presence, giving to him. What do we give him? Through our words and thoughts we can give to him honour, adoration, attention, praise and worship.

If this is difficult for you I suggest you go through your Bible underlining the passages that specifically speak about the character of God. The Psalms are a good place to begin. Then pray and sing those passages to the Father in your times of prayer. As you do this daily you will find yourself growing in love with the Father. You will find him speaking intimately to you in response to your words of praise. Do not be surprised when he speaks words of appreciation, approval and love throughout the day. He loves to love his children!

Step 6: Think God's thoughts

In response to the hurtful things that are said and done to us, especially as children, we build destructive habits of thinking about ourselves. For example, if your parents were perfectionists and very demanding, you could have often failed to live up to their expectations. One way of responding to this could be to programme yourself for failure. If you 'know' you will fail, then you are in a way trying to protect yourself from disappointment. Unfortunately, if you think you will fail, you often will. Such negative thought patterns are often not accurate or kind. They are built on fear or are born out of rejection. If you think you are ugly, you will not only feel that way, you will also act that way.

The Bible says we should love God with all our heart,

soul, mind and body, and that we should love our neighbour *as ourselves* (Lev 19:18, Mt. 19:19). God wants us to love ourselves, not selfishly, but with his love. He wants us to think his thoughts about ourselves – thoughts of kindness, esteem, respect and trust.

If you have negative thought patterns about yourself, I would like you to stop now and write down the two or three negative ways of thinking that are most common. After you have done that, write down God's thoughts towards you that are the opposite of the negative thoughts, based on God's word or character. For example, if you wrote down that you think you will always fail, write opposite that 'I am good at . . .' and name one thing you do well. Also write down what the Bible says about that area of your life. For example, 'I can do all things in him who strengthens me' (Phil 4:13). *Every time you start to think the negative thought, stop and say the positive thought along with the scripture.* It may take a long time to break a bad habit and replace it with a good one. Keep telling yourself the truth until you have broken the negative habit. Don't give in to lies and condemning thoughts. Persevere – with God's help you can do it. Cry out to him each time you fail, and start again. Have you ever noticed in the Bible how often God repeats something to somebody when he is trying to encourage them? In chapter 1 of the book of Joshua, the Lord tells Joshua *four* times not to be afraid. Why? Because Joshua needed to be encouraged to think God's thoughts about himself. He was getting ready to go into battle and he needed that encouragement. I am sure he must have repeated those words of the Lord to himself over and over again.

The most common cause of depression is thinking thoughts of depreciation and condemnation about ourselves. To break this cause of depression we need to follow the steps I have outlined above and then *get sick and tired of being tired and sick!* We need to break the habit of negative thinking by thinking God's thoughts.

This same principle also applies to reactions that go beyond our thoughts, to our actions. As you become aware of certain 'reaction patterns' in your life that are negative, defensive or selfish, write them down. Then beside them write down how God wants you to react in the situations that cause you to be threatened or defensive. When you find yourself acting in a negative or selfish way, stop and pray; then choose the way you know God wants you to respond.

In prayer, ask God to enable you to put these thoughts and choices into action. When you fail, ask for his forgiveness and keep going. If the devil tells you you have 'failed again' agree with him, but tell him you refuse to feel sorry for yourself! Accept responsibility for your failure, ask God's forgiveness or help, and continue doing this. Keep working away at it until you have established new habits of righteousness. It took you years to develop the negative habits, so don't give up because it takes a few weeks or months to replace them with God's habits. Start with one or two at a time, and then go on to others. As we do the possible, God will do the impossible.

Step 7: Endurance

Ninety per cent of success is finishing! The Bible says those 'who endure to the end will be saved' (Mt 10:22), and 'If we endure, we shall also reign with him' (2 Tim 2:12). Endurance has two aspects: on the one side it means the commitment on our part not to give up, a determination to go all the way through; on the other side it has to do with God's enablement. What God calls us to do, he gives us the grace to accomplish. His commands are at the same time his promise of victory. If he says, 'You shall be holy, for I am holy (1 Pet 1:16), that is not only a command, but also a promise – you *shall* be holy!

Sometimes you might feel it's impossible to go through to the end, to endure. And that may be right! But when we come to the end of what is possible for us, then we can see God do the impossible. Faith has not begun until we believe God for the impossible. We don't need faith to do what is possible. So if you are facing impossible situations in your life, praise God. Now you can begin to exercise your faith.

It is like climbing out on the limb of a tree for God, when you trust for something impossible. You are stepping out in a precarious situation where you know you need help. If you are overwhelmed with your needs or problems or the impossible situation you face, the devil loves to come along and tell you it won't work, that you cannot make it. 'The limb will break off,' he says repeatedly. So there you are out on that limb and what does the devil do? He starts cutting the limb off! He not only predicts it will break off, he tries to fulfil his own prediction! But stay right there and hang on to the Lord. When the devil cuts the limb off, the tree will fall on the devil and the limb will stay right up there in the air!

Why is endurance a step in God's healing process in our lives? It is giving up that allows us to give in to resentment, anger, hurt, rejection, lust, a critical nature, mistrust or whatever may be plaguing us. Sometimes we want God to perform a miracle and take away all our problems *right now*. But God is leading us in a process that is preparing us ultimately to reign with him in heaven. So we need to build character, and that comes through enduring difficulties or temptations and making the right choices.

Heaven is not just angels playing harps and living in big mansions. God wants us to rule with him. He has a part for each of us in ruling over his creation. But that begins in a relationship with him here on earth. The Father is preparing us as his children to share with him in ruling over all his creation. How will we do that? I don't know. But scriptures like the one in 2 Corinthians 4:16–18 confirm that God is preparing us for eternity: 'So we do not lose heart. Though our outer nature is wasting away, our inner nature is being renewed every day. For this slight momentary affliction is preparing for us an eternal weight of glory beyond all comparison.'

As a friend of mine says, 'It's how you finish that counts!' The apostle Paul says in his first letter to the Corinthian church, 'Do you not know that in a race all the runners compete, but only one receives the prize? So run that you may obtain it. Every athlete exercises self-control in all things. They do it to receive a perishable wreath, but we an imperishable. Well, I do not run aimlessly, I do not box as one beating the air; but I pommel my body and subdue it, lest after preaching to others I myself should be disqualified' (1 Cor 9:24–27).

There have been times when I have failed in an area of my life in which I am really struggling, and the devil comes along and says to me, 'You've failed again. You'll never make it. It's too difficult.' He tries to discourage me to the point of totally giving up.

Now if you stop to think about it, there is some truth in those thoughts. So I have learned to say to the enemy, 'That's right, I have failed again. But it is my responsibility. I accept my responsibility for what I have done. Thank you for reminding me of that. But I refuse to have self-pity over my failures. And you're right too, when you say I can't make it. By myself I cannot. But I can do all things through Christ who strengthens me. I am weak, but he is strong. Greater is he who is in me than you who are in the world.'

Then I rebuke him and his thoughts of defeat in the name of Jesus Christ and I begin to pray to the Lord. I confess my sin to the Lord and I refuse to feel sorry for myself. The cure for self-pity is confession of sin, turning away from the sin, and receiving the Lord's forgiveness.

As we confess our sins, turn away from them and choose to hate them as an act of faith, we receive God's forgiveness and God gives us a new beginning. *He is the God of new beginnings.* Our part is to humble ourselves and turn away from our sin or failure, his part is to forgive us and give us a new beginning. He loves to do that, because he is a God of love. It is pride not to receive his forgiveness if we have 'failed again'. If we've failed, we've failed; we must be honest and admit it, humble ourselves before God, and receive his forgiveness.

He is at work in you. *The struggle is part of the victory process.* You are learning lessons: you are learning to humble yourself; you are learning to receive forgiveness; you are learning endurance; you are learning from your mistakes and failures; you are learning how to help others and you are learning to fight the enemy.

We are at war! Don't give up! You are on the winning side!

And I am sure that he who began a good work in you will bring it to completion at the day of Jesus Christ . . . .

THE COMPASSIONATE FATHER

Therefore, my beloved, as you have always obeyed, so now, not only as in my presence but much more in my absence, work out your own salvation with fear and trembling; for God is at work in you, both to will and to work for his good pleasure.... I can do all things in him who strengthens me... and my God will supply every need of yours according to his riches in Christ Jesus.... Likewise the Spirit helps us in our weakness; for we do not know how to pray as we ought, but the Spirit himself intercedes for us with sighs too deep for words.... What then shall we say to this? If God is for us, who is against us? He who did not spare his own Son but gave him up for us all, will he not also give us all things with him?.... Who shall separate us from the love of Christ? Shall tribulation, or distress, or persecution, or famine, or nakedness, or peril, or sword? As it is written, 'For thy sake we are being killed all the day long; we are regarded as sheep to be slaughtered.' No, in all these things we are more than conquerors through him who loved us. For I am sure that neither death, nor life, nor angels, nor principalities, nor things present, nor things to come, nor powers, nor height, nor depth, nor anything else in all creation, will be able to separate us from the love of God in Christ Jesus our Lord.

(Phil 1:6; 2:12–13; 4:13,19; Rom 8:26, 31–32, 35–39)